found, please notify owner.
ntact information on page 6.

LOGBOOK NO: _____

FROM: _____

TO: _____

GLEIM® | Aviation
PILOT LOGBOOK

GLEIM® PILOT LOGBOOK

ISBN 978-1-58194-574-4

Copyright © 2019 Gleim Publications, Inc. Portions of this work were first published in the U.S. as *Gleim Pilot Logboo* copyright © 2002 by Irvin N. Gleim.

Gleim Publications, Inc.

PO Box 12848 • University Station
Gainesville, FL 32604

352.375.0772
800.874.5346
352.375.6940 (FAX)

GleimAviation.com
aviationteam@gleim.com

TABLE OF CONTENTS

HOW TO USE THIS LOGBOOK TO COMPLETE YOUR
AIRMAN CERTIFICATE AND/OR RATING APPLICATION (FAA FORM 8710-1)

All pilots are required to complete FAA Form 8710-1, *Airman Certificate and/or Rating Application*, prior to taking the practical test for a new certificate or rating. Section III of the form is a record of your total pilot experience obtained to date. This section requires you to provide certain information that is specific to the requirements for obtaining various certificates and ratings but is not normally used for other purposes.

	Total	Instruction Received	Solo	Pilot in Command (PIC)	Cross Country Instruction Received	Cross Country Solo	Cross Country PIC	Instrument	Night Instruction Received	Night Take-Off/ Landings	Night PIC	Night Take-Off/ Landing PIC	Number of Flights	Number of Aero-Tows	Number of Ground Launches	Number of Power Launch
Airplanes				PIC		PIC					PIC	PIC				
				SIC		SIC					SIC	SIC				

The major disadvantage of most logbooks is that the information required to complete the *Airman Certificate and/or Rating Application* must be obtained by carefully analyzing each entry in the logbook to pick out the data needed, which are not recorded in the regular logbook columns. As your total flight experience increases, this process becomes increasingly laborious due to the sheer volume of data that must be analyzed.

Your workload and the number of potential errors can be greatly reduced if this data is summarized at the completion of each individual page. Each page's totals can then be added to the totals obtained to date and carried forward to the next page, in the same manner that is used to keep up with your other flight experience. Accordingly, we have included a separate section on each logbook page for the purpose of keeping track of information that is specific to Section III of FAA Form 8710-1. The "8710-1 Information" section will allow you to keep up with the specialized data necessary to complete your application without decreasing the general utility of the logbook.

8710-1 INFORMATION	XC INST'N REC'D		XC SOLO		XC PIC		NIGHT INST'N REC'D		NIGHT PIC		NIGHT T/O & LDGS PIC	
	1.		**2.**		**3.**		**4.**		**5.**		**6.**	
Page Total												
Previous Total												
Total to Date												

To complete the 8710-1 section on each page, analyze each entry (NOT column) in order to determine the total number of plicable flight hours or takeoffs and landings, and record them on the "Page Total" line for each of the categories listed below:

Cross-Country (XC) Instruction Received time is all time in the "Over 50 NM" column that is also recorded in the "Flight Training Received" column.
Cross-Country Solo time is all time in the "Over 50 NM" column that is also recorded in the "Solo" column.
Cross-Country PIC time is all time in the "Over 50 NM" column that is also recorded in the "PIC" column.
Night Instruction Received time is all time in the "Night" column that is also recorded in the "Flight Training Received" column.
Night PIC time is all time in the "Night" column that is also recorded in the "PIC" column.
Night Takeoffs and Landings as PIC are all night landings made during flight time recorded in the "PIC" column.

When completing the 8710-1 section, be sure to always use the times (as described above) for each individual entry. DO NOT e the totals for each column, as errors may result.
Please email us at aviationteam@gleim.com if you have any questions about this or any other product.

Pilot Information

ATTENTION: There is a reward for the return of this logbook.

Name: _____

Mailing Address: _____

_____

Telephone 1: _____ Telephone 2: _____ Email: _____

Medical Certificates							
Date	Class	Name of Aviation Medical Examiner	Expiration Date	Date	Class	Name of Aviation Medical Examiner	Expiration D

Certificates, Ratings, and Operating Privileges Earned

Certificates			Ratings		Operating Privileges		
ertificate	Issue Date	Certificate Number	Rating	Issue Date	Privilege	Endorsement Date	Expiration Date
udent			Airplane Single-Engine Land		90-Day Student Solo		
ort			Airplane Multi-Engine Land		90-Day Student Solo		
ght Instructor with Sport Pilot Rating			Instrument		90-Day Student Solo		
ecreational			Instrument Instructor (CFII)		Night Student Solo		
ivate			Multi-Engine Instructor (MEI)		Student Solo in Class B		
ommercial					Student Solo at an Airport in Class B		
ght Instructor					Student Solo in Class B, C, and/or D (Sport Pilot)		
ound Instructor					Complex Airplane		
rline Transport Pilot					High-Performance Airplane		
					Tailwheel Airplane		
					High-Altitude Pressurized Airplane		

DATE 20___	MAKE AND MODEL	ID NUMBER	FROM	TO	LANDINGS		INSTRUMENT APPROACHES		AIRCRAFT CATEGORY AND CLASS				INSTRUMENT		
					DAY	NT	NO.	TYPE & LOCATION	AIRPLANE SINGLE	AIRPLANE MULTI			ACTUAL	SIMULATED (HOOD)	FTD OR SIMULAT
I certify that all information contained in this flight record is true. Pilot's Signature: _____			Page Total												
			Previous Total												
			Total to Date												

8

NIGHT		CROSS COUNTRY				PIC		SOLO		GROUND TRAINING RECEIVED		FLIGHT TRAINING RECEIVED		FLIGHT TRAINING GIVEN		TOTAL FLIGHT TIME		REMARKS
		ALL		OVER 50 NM														

8710-1 INFORMATION	XC INST'N REC'D		XC SOLO		XC PIC		NIGHT INST'N REC'D		NIGHT PIC		NIGHT T/O & LDGS PIC	
Page Total												
Previous Total												
Total to Date												

Instructions for use on page 5.

DATE 20___	MAKE AND MODEL	ID NUMBER	FROM	TO	LANDINGS		INSTRUMENT APPROACHES		AIRCRAFT CATEGORY AND CLASS					INSTRUMENT		
					DAY	NT	NO.	TYPE & LOCATION	AIRPLANE SINGLE	AIRPLANE MULTI			ACTUAL	SIMULATED (HOOD)	FTD OR SIMULAT
I certify that all information contained in this flight record is true. Pilot's Signature: _____			Page Total												
			Previous Total												
			Total to Date												

IGHT		CROSS COUNTRY		PIC		SOLO		GROUND TRAINING RECEIVED		FLIGHT TRAINING RECEIVED		FLIGHT TRAINING GIVEN		TOTAL FLIGHT TIME		REMARKS
		ALL	OVER 50 NM													

8710-1 INFORMATION	XC INST'N REC'D	XC SOLO	XC PIC	NIGHT INST'N REC'D	NIGHT PIC	NIGHT T/O & LDGS PIC
Page Total						
Previous Total						
Total to Date						

11

DATE 20___	MAKE AND MODEL	ID NUMBER	FROM	TO	LANDINGS		INSTRUMENT APPROACHES		AIRCRAFT CATEGORY AND CLASS				INSTRUMENT		
					DAY	NT	NO.	TYPE & LOCATION	AIRPLANE SINGLE	AIRPLANE MULTI			ACTUAL	SIMULATED (HOOD)	FTD OR SIMULAT
I certify that all information contained in this flight record is true. Pilot's Signature: _____			Page Total												
			Previous Total												
			Total to Date												

12

NIGHT	CROSS COUNTRY		PIC	SOLO	GROUND TRAINING RECEIVED	FLIGHT TRAINING RECEIVED	FLIGHT TRAINING GIVEN	TOTAL FLIGHT TIME	REMARKS
	ALL	OVER 50 NM							

8710-1 INFORMATION	XC INST'N REC'D	XC SOLO	XC PIC	NIGHT INST'N REC'D	NIGHT PIC	NIGHT T/O & LDGS PIC
Page Total						
Previous Total						
Total to Date						

DATE 20___	MAKE AND MODEL	ID NUMBER	FROM	TO	LANDINGS		INSTRUMENT APPROACHES		AIRCRAFT CATEGORY AND CLASS				INSTRUMENT		
					DAY	NT	NO.	TYPE & LOCATION	AIRPLANE SINGLE	AIRPLANE MULTI			ACTUAL	SIMULATED (HOOD)	FTD OF SIMULAT
I certify that all information contained in this flight record is true. Pilot's Signature: _____			Page Total												
			Previous Total												
			Total to Date												

14

NIGHT		CROSS COUNTRY			PIC		SOLO		GROUND TRAINING RECEIVED		FLIGHT TRAINING RECEIVED		FLIGHT TRAINING GIVEN		TOTAL FLIGHT TIME		REMARKS
		ALL		OVER 50 NM														

8710-1 INFORMATION	XC INST'N REC'D		XC SOLO		XC PIC		NIGHT INST'N REC'D		NIGHT PIC		NIGHT T/O & LDGS PIC
Page Total											
Previous Total											
Total to Date											

15

DATE 20___	MAKE AND MODEL	ID NUMBER	FROM	TO	LANDINGS		INSTRUMENT APPROACHES		AIRCRAFT CATEGORY AND CLASS				INSTRUMENT		
					DAY	NT	NO.	TYPE & LOCATION	AIRPLANE SINGLE	AIRPLANE MULTI			ACTUAL	SIMULATED (HOOD)	FTD OR SIMULAT

I certify that all information contained in this flight record is true.

Pilot's Signature:

_____

Page Total				
Previous Total				
Total to Date				

NIGHT	CROSS COUNTRY			PIC	SOLO	GROUND TRAINING RECEIVED	FLIGHT TRAINING RECEIVED	FLIGHT TRAINING GIVEN	TOTAL FLIGHT TIME	REMARKS
	ALL		OVER 50 NM							

8710-1 INFORMATION	XC INST'N REC'D	XC SOLO	XC PIC	NIGHT INST'N REC'D	NIGHT PIC	NIGHT T/O & LDGS PIC
Page Total						
Previous Total						
Total to Date						

17

DATE 20___	MAKE AND MODEL	ID NUMBER	FROM	TO	LANDINGS		INSTRUMENT APPROACHES		AIRCRAFT CATEGORY AND CLASS				INSTRUMENT		
					DAY	NT	NO.	TYPE & LOCATION	AIRPLANE SINGLE	AIRPLANE MULTI			ACTUAL	SIMULATED (HOOD)	FTD OR SIMULAT

I certify that all information contained in this flight record is true.

Pilot's Signature:

_____

	Page Total													
	Previous Total													
	Total to Date													

NIGHT		CROSS COUNTRY		PIC		SOLO		GROUND TRAINING RECEIVED		FLIGHT TRAINING RECEIVED		FLIGHT TRAINING GIVEN		TOTAL FLIGHT TIME		REMARKS
		ALL	OVER 50 NM													

8710-1 INFORMATION	XC INST'N REC'D		XC SOLO		XC PIC		NIGHT INST'N REC'D		NIGHT PIC		NIGHT T/O & LDGS PIC	
Page Total												
Previous Total												
Total to Date												

| DATE 20___ | MAKE AND MODEL | ID NUMBER | FROM | TO | LANDINGS | | INSTRUMENT APPROACHES | | AIRCRAFT CATEGORY AND CLASS | | | | | INSTRUMENT | | |
					DAY	NT	NO.	TYPE & LOCATION	AIRPLANE SINGLE	AIRPLANE MULTI				ACTUAL	SIMULATED (HOOD)	FTD OR SIMULATO
I certify that all information contained in this flight record is true. Pilot's Signature: _____			Page Total													
			Previous Total													
			Total to Date													

IGHT		CROSS COUNTRY		PIC		SOLO		GROUND TRAINING RECEIVED		FLIGHT TRAINING RECEIVED		FLIGHT TRAINING GIVEN		TOTAL FLIGHT TIME		REMARKS
		ALL	OVER 50 NM													

8710-1 INFORMATION	XC INST'N REC'D		XC SOLO		XC PIC		NIGHT INST'N REC'D		NIGHT PIC		NIGHT T/O & LDGS PIC	
Page Total												
Previous Total												
Total to Date												

DATE 20___	MAKE AND MODEL	ID NUMBER	FROM	TO	LANDINGS		INSTRUMENT APPROACHES		AIRCRAFT CATEGORY AND CLASS					INSTRUMENT		
					DAY	NT	NO.	TYPE & LOCATION	AIRPLANE SINGLE	AIRPLANE MULTI				ACTUAL	SIMULATED (HOOD)	FTD OR SIMULAT

I certify that all information contained in this flight record is true. Pilot's Signature: _____	Page Total														
	Previous Total														
	Total to Date														

| IGHT | CROSS COUNTRY | | PIC | SOLO | GROUND TRAINING RECEIVED | FLIGHT TRAINING RECEIVED | FLIGHT TRAINING GIVEN | TOTAL FLIGHT TIME | REMARKS |
	ALL	OVER 50 NM							

8710-1 INFORMATION	XC INST'N REC'D	XC SOLO	XC PIC	NIGHT INST'N REC'D	NIGHT PIC	NIGHT T/O & LDGS PIC
Page Total						
Previous Total						
Total to Date						

DATE 20___	MAKE AND MODEL	ID NUMBER	FROM	TO	LANDINGS		INSTRUMENT APPROACHES		AIRCRAFT CATEGORY AND CLASS				INSTRUMENT		
					DAY	NT	NO.	TYPE & LOCATION	AIRPLANE SINGLE	AIRPLANE MULTI			ACTUAL	SIMULATED (HOOD)	FTD OF SIMULAT

I certify that all information contained in this flight record is true.

Pilot's Signature:

_____

Page Total								
Previous Total								
Total to Date								

| NIGHT | CROSS COUNTRY | | PIC | SOLO | GROUND TRAINING RECEIVED | FLIGHT TRAINING RECEIVED | FLIGHT TRAINING GIVEN | TOTAL FLIGHT TIME | REMARKS |
	ALL	OVER 50 NM							

									8710-1 INFORMATION	XC INST'N REC'D	XC SOLO	XC PIC	NIGHT INST'N REC'D	NIGHT PIC	NIGHT T/O & LDGS PIC
									Page Total						
									Previous Total						
									Total to Date						

DATE 20___	MAKE AND MODEL	ID NUMBER	FROM	TO	LANDINGS		INSTRUMENT APPROACHES		AIRCRAFT CATEGORY AND CLASS				INSTRUMENT		
					DAY	NT	NO.	TYPE & LOCATION	AIRPLANE SINGLE	AIRPLANE MULTI			ACTUAL	SIMULATED (HOOD)	FTD OR SIMULAT

I certify that all information contained in this flight record is true. Pilot's Signature: _____	Page Total												
	Previous Total												
	Total to Date												

IGHT		CROSS COUNTRY		PIC		SOLO		GROUND TRAINING RECEIVED		FLIGHT TRAINING RECEIVED		FLIGHT TRAINING GIVEN		TOTAL FLIGHT TIME		REMARKS
		ALL	OVER 50 NM													

8710-1 INFORMATION	XC INST'N REC'D		XC SOLO		XC PIC		NIGHT INST'N REC'D		NIGHT PIC		NIGHT T/O & LDGS PIC	
Page Total												
Previous Total												
Total to Date												

27

DATE 20___	MAKE AND MODEL	ID NUMBER	FROM	TO	LANDINGS		INSTRUMENT APPROACHES		AIRCRAFT CATEGORY AND CLASS				INSTRUMENT		
					DAY	NT	NO.	TYPE & LOCATION	AIRPLANE SINGLE	AIRPLANE MULTI			ACTUAL	SIMULATED (HOOD)	FTD O SIMULAT
I certify that all information contained in this flight record is true. Pilot's Signature: _____			Page Total												
			Previous Total												
			Total to Date												

NIGHT		CROSS COUNTRY		PIC		SOLO		GROUND TRAINING RECEIVED		FLIGHT TRAINING RECEIVED		FLIGHT TRAINING GIVEN		TOTAL FLIGHT TIME		REMARKS
		ALL	OVER 50 NM													

8710-1 INFORMATION	XC INST'N REC'D		XC SOLO		XC PIC		NIGHT INST'N REC'D		NIGHT PIC		NIGHT T/O & LDGS PIC	
Page Total												
Previous Total												
Total to Date												

DATE 20___	MAKE AND MODEL	ID NUMBER	FROM	TO	LANDINGS		INSTRUMENT APPROACHES		AIRCRAFT CATEGORY AND CLASS					INSTRUMENT		
					DAY	NT	NO.	TYPE & LOCATION	AIRPLANE SINGLE	AIRPLANE MULTI				ACTUAL	SIMULATED (HOOD)	FTD O SIMULAT
I certify that all information contained in this flight record is true. Pilot's Signature: _____			Page Total													
			Previous Total													
			Total to Date													

NIGHT	CROSS COUNTRY		PIC	SOLO	GROUND TRAINING RECEIVED	FLIGHT TRAINING RECEIVED	FLIGHT TRAINING GIVEN	TOTAL FLIGHT TIME	REMARKS
	ALL	OVER 50 NM							

8710-1 INFORMATION	XC INST'N REC'D	XC SOLO	XC PIC	NIGHT INST'N REC'D	NIGHT PIC	NIGHT T/O & LDGS PIC
Page Total						
Previous Total						
Total to Date						

31

DATE 20___	MAKE AND MODEL	ID NUMBER	FROM	TO	LANDINGS		INSTRUMENT APPROACHES		AIRCRAFT CATEGORY AND CLASS				INSTRUMENT		
					DAY	NT	NO.	TYPE & LOCATION	AIRPLANE SINGLE	AIRPLANE MULTI			ACTUAL	SIMULATED (HOOD)	FTD OR SIMULAT

I certify that all information contained in this flight record is true. Pilot's Signature: _____	Page Total										
	Previous Total										
	Total to Date										

32

IGHT	CROSS COUNTRY		PIC	SOLO	GROUND TRAINING RECEIVED	FLIGHT TRAINING RECEIVED	FLIGHT TRAINING GIVEN	TOTAL FLIGHT TIME	REMARKS
	ALL	OVER 50 NM							

									8710-1 INFORMATION	XC INST'N REC'D	XC SOLO	XC PIC	NIGHT INST'N REC'D	NIGHT PIC	NIGHT T/O & LDGS PIC
									Page Total						
									Previous Total						
									Total to Date						

33

DATE 20___	MAKE AND MODEL	ID NUMBER	FROM	TO	LANDINGS		INSTRUMENT APPROACHES		AIRCRAFT CATEGORY AND CLASS				INSTRUMENT		
					DAY	NT	NO.	TYPE & LOCATION	AIRPLANE SINGLE	AIRPLANE MULTI			ACTUAL	SIMULATED (HOOD)	FTD O SIMULAT
I certify that all information contained in this flight record is true. Pilot's Signature: _____			Page Total												
			Previous Total												
			Total to Date												

34

| NIGHT | CROSS COUNTRY | | PIC | SOLO | GROUND TRAINING RECEIVED | FLIGHT TRAINING RECEIVED | FLIGHT TRAINING GIVEN | TOTAL FLIGHT TIME | REMARKS |
	ALL	OVER 50 NM							

8710-1 INFORMATION	XC INST'N REC'D	XC SOLO	XC PIC	NIGHT INST'N REC'D	NIGHT PIC	NIGHT T/O & LDGS PIC
Page Total						
Previous Total						
Total to Date						

DATE 20___	MAKE AND MODEL	ID NUMBER	FROM	TO	LANDINGS		INSTRUMENT APPROACHES		AIRCRAFT CATEGORY AND CLASS				INSTRUMENT		
					DAY	NT	NO.	TYPE & LOCATION	AIRPLANE SINGLE	AIRPLANE MULTI			ACTUAL	SIMULATED (HOOD)	FTD OR SIMULAT

I certify that all information contained in this flight record is true.

Pilot's Signature:

_____

Page Total	
Previous Total	
Total to Date	

IGHT	CROSS COUNTRY		PIC	SOLO	GROUND TRAINING RECEIVED	FLIGHT TRAINING RECEIVED	FLIGHT TRAINING GIVEN	TOTAL FLIGHT TIME	REMARKS
	ALL	OVER 50 NM							

8710-1 INFORMATION	XC INST'N REC'D	XC SOLO	XC PIC	NIGHT INST'N REC'D	NIGHT PIC	NIGHT T/O & LDGS PIC
Page Total						
Previous Total						
Total to Date						

DATE 20___	MAKE AND MODEL	ID NUMBER	FROM	TO	LANDINGS		INSTRUMENT APPROACHES		AIRCRAFT CATEGORY AND CLASS				INSTRUMENT		
					DAY	NT	NO.	TYPE & LOCATION	AIRPLANE SINGLE	AIRPLANE MULTI			ACTUAL	SIMULATED (HOOD)	FTD O SIMULAT
I certify that all information contained in this flight record is true. Pilot's Signature: _____			Page Total												
			Previous Total												
			Total to Date												

NIGHT		CROSS COUNTRY		PIC		SOLO		GROUND TRAINING RECEIVED		FLIGHT TRAINING RECEIVED		FLIGHT TRAINING GIVEN		TOTAL FLIGHT TIME		REMARKS
		ALL	OVER 50 NM													

8710-1 INFORMATION	XC INST'N REC'D		XC SOLO		XC PIC		NIGHT INST'N REC'D		NIGHT PIC		NIGHT T/O & LDGS PIC	
Page Total												
Previous Total												
Total to Date												

DATE 20___	MAKE AND MODEL	ID NUMBER	FROM	TO	LANDINGS		INSTRUMENT APPROACHES		AIRCRAFT CATEGORY AND CLASS				INSTRUMENT		
					DAY	NT	NO.	TYPE & LOCATION	AIRPLANE SINGLE	AIRPLANE MULTI			ACTUAL	SIMULATED (HOOD)	FTD O SIMULAT

I certify that all information contained in this flight record is true.

Pilot's Signature:

_____

Page Total			
Previous Total			
Total to Date			

NIGHT		CROSS COUNTRY		PIC		SOLO		GROUND TRAINING RECEIVED		FLIGHT TRAINING RECEIVED		FLIGHT TRAINING GIVEN		TOTAL FLIGHT TIME		REMARKS
		ALL	OVER 50 NM													

8710-1 INFORMATION	XC INST'N REC'D	XC SOLO	XC PIC	NIGHT INST'N REC'D	NIGHT PIC	NIGHT T/O & LDGS PIC
Page Total						
Previous Total						
Total to Date						

DATE 20___	MAKE AND MODEL	ID NUMBER	FROM	TO	LANDINGS		INSTRUMENT APPROACHES		AIRCRAFT CATEGORY AND CLASS				INSTRUMENT		
					DAY	NT	NO.	TYPE & LOCATION	AIRPLANE SINGLE	AIRPLANE MULTI			ACTUAL	SIMULATED (HOOD)	FTD OR SIMULAT
I certify that all information contained in this flight record is true. Pilot's Signature: _____			Page Total												
			Previous Total												
			Total to Date												

IGHT		CROSS COUNTRY		PIC	SOLO	GROUND TRAINING RECEIVED	FLIGHT TRAINING RECEIVED	FLIGHT TRAINING GIVEN	TOTAL FLIGHT TIME	REMARKS
		ALL	OVER 50 NM							

										8710-1 INFORMATION	XC INST'N REC'D	XC SOLO	XC PIC	NIGHT INST'N REC'D	NIGHT PIC	NIGHT T/O & LDGS PIC
										Page Total						
										Previous Total						
										Total to Date						

DATE 20___	MAKE AND MODEL	ID NUMBER	FROM	TO	LANDINGS		INSTRUMENT APPROACHES		AIRCRAFT CATEGORY AND CLASS				INSTRUMENT		
					DAY	NT	NO.	TYPE & LOCATION	AIRPLANE SINGLE	AIRPLANE MULTI			ACTUAL	SIMULATED (HOOD)	FTD OR SIMULAT
I certify that all information contained in this flight record is true. Pilot's Signature: _____			Page Total												
			Previous Total												
			Total to Date												

44

NIGHT	CROSS COUNTRY		PIC	SOLO	GROUND TRAINING RECEIVED	FLIGHT TRAINING RECEIVED	FLIGHT TRAINING GIVEN	TOTAL FLIGHT TIME	REMARKS
	ALL	OVER 50 NM							

8710-1 INFORMATION	XC INST'N REC'D	XC SOLO	XC PIC	NIGHT INST'N REC'D	NIGHT PIC	NIGHT T/O & LDGS PIC
Page Total						
Previous Total						
Total to Date						

45

DATE 20___	MAKE AND MODEL	ID NUMBER	FROM	TO	LANDINGS		INSTRUMENT APPROACHES		AIRCRAFT CATEGORY AND CLASS				INSTRUMENT		
					DAY	NT	NO.	TYPE & LOCATION	AIRPLANE SINGLE	AIRPLANE MULTI			ACTUAL	SIMULATED (HOOD)	FTD O SIMULAT
I certify that all information contained in this flight record is true. Pilot's Signature: _____			Page Total												
			Previous Total												
			Total to Date												

46

| NIGHT | CROSS COUNTRY | | PIC | SOLO | GROUND TRAINING RECEIVED | FLIGHT TRAINING RECEIVED | FLIGHT TRAINING GIVEN | TOTAL FLIGHT TIME | REMARKS |
	ALL	OVER 50 NM							

8710-1 INFORMATION	XC INST'N REC'D	XC SOLO	XC PIC	NIGHT INST'N REC'D	NIGHT PIC	NIGHT T/O & LDGS PIC
Page Total						
Previous Total						
Total to Date						

| DATE 20___ | MAKE AND MODEL | ID NUMBER | FROM | TO | LANDINGS | | INSTRUMENT APPROACHES | | AIRCRAFT CATEGORY AND CLASS | | | | INSTRUMENT | | |
					DAY	NT	NO.	TYPE & LOCATION	AIRPLANE SINGLE	AIRPLANE MULTI			ACTUAL	SIMULATED (HOOD)	FTD OF SIMULAT

I certify that all information contained in this flight record is true.

Pilot's Signature:

_____

	Page Total												
	Previous Total												
	Total to Date												

| NIGHT | CROSS COUNTRY | | PIC | SOLO | GROUND TRAINING RECEIVED | FLIGHT TRAINING RECEIVED | FLIGHT TRAINING GIVEN | TOTAL FLIGHT TIME | REMARKS |
	ALL	OVER 50 NM							

8710-1 INFORMATION	XC INST'N REC'D	XC SOLO	XC PIC	NIGHT INST'N REC'D	NIGHT PIC	NIGHT T/O & LDGS PIC
Page Total						
Previous Total						
Total to Date						

DATE 20___	MAKE AND MODEL	ID NUMBER	FROM	TO	LANDINGS		INSTRUMENT APPROACHES		AIRCRAFT CATEGORY AND CLASS				INSTRUMENT		
					DAY	NT	NO.	TYPE & LOCATION	AIRPLANE SINGLE	AIRPLANE MULTI			ACTUAL	SIMULATED (HOOD)	FTD OF SIMULAT

I certify that all information contained in this flight record is true. Pilot's Signature: _____	Page Total												
	Previous Total												
	Total to Date												

NIGHT	CROSS COUNTRY		PIC	SOLO	GROUND TRAINING RECEIVED	FLIGHT TRAINING RECEIVED	FLIGHT TRAINING GIVEN	TOTAL FLIGHT TIME	REMARKS
	ALL	OVER 50 NM							

									8710-1 INFORMATION	XC INST'N REC'D	XC SOLO	XC PIC	NIGHT INST'N REC'D	NIGHT PIC	NIGHT T/O & LDGS PIC
									Page Total						
									Previous Total						
									Total to Date						

DATE 20___	MAKE AND MODEL	ID NUMBER	FROM	TO	LANDINGS		INSTRUMENT APPROACHES		AIRCRAFT CATEGORY AND CLASS				INSTRUMENT		
					DAY	NT	NO.	TYPE & LOCATION	AIRPLANE SINGLE	AIRPLANE MULTI			ACTUAL	SIMULATED (HOOD)	FTD OR SIMULAT
I certify that all information contained in this flight record is true. Pilot's Signature: _____			Page Total												
			Previous Total												
			Total to Date												

NIGHT		CROSS COUNTRY		PIC		SOLO		GROUND TRAINING RECEIVED		FLIGHT TRAINING RECEIVED		FLIGHT TRAINING GIVEN		TOTAL FLIGHT TIME		REMARKS
		ALL	OVER 50 NM													

8710-1 INFORMATION	XC INST'N REC'D		XC SOLO		XC PIC		NIGHT INST'N REC'D		NIGHT PIC		NIGHT T/O & LDGS PIC	
Page Total												
Previous Total												
Total to Date												

DATE 20___	MAKE AND MODEL	ID NUMBER	FROM	TO	LANDINGS		INSTRUMENT APPROACHES		AIRCRAFT CATEGORY AND CLASS				INSTRUMENT		
					DAY	NT	NO.	TYPE & LOCATION	AIRPLANE SINGLE	AIRPLANE MULTI			ACTUAL	SIMULATED (HOOD)	FTD OR SIMULAT
I certify that all information contained in this flight record is true. Pilot's Signature: _____			Page Total												
			Previous Total												
			Total to Date												

NIGHT	CROSS COUNTRY		PIC	SOLO	GROUND TRAINING RECEIVED	FLIGHT TRAINING RECEIVED	FLIGHT TRAINING GIVEN	TOTAL FLIGHT TIME	REMARKS
	ALL	OVER 50 NM							

8710-1 INFORMATION	XC INST'N REC'D	XC SOLO	XC PIC	NIGHT INST'N REC'D	NIGHT PIC	NIGHT T/O & LDGS PIC
Page Total						
Previous Total						
Total to Date						

DATE 20___	MAKE AND MODEL	ID NUMBER	FROM	TO	LANDINGS		INSTRUMENT APPROACHES		AIRCRAFT CATEGORY AND CLASS				INSTRUMENT		
					DAY	NT	NO.	TYPE & LOCATION	AIRPLANE SINGLE	AIRPLANE MULTI			ACTUAL	SIMULATED (HOOD)	FTD OR SIMULAT
I certify that all information contained in this flight record is true. Pilot's Signature: _____			Page Total												
			Previous Total												
			Total to Date												

56

NIGHT	CROSS COUNTRY		PIC	SOLO	GROUND TRAINING RECEIVED	FLIGHT TRAINING RECEIVED	FLIGHT TRAINING GIVEN	TOTAL FLIGHT TIME	REMARKS
	ALL	OVER 50 NM							

8710-1 INFORMATION	XC INST'N REC'D	XC SOLO	XC PIC	NIGHT INST'N REC'D	NIGHT PIC	NIGHT T/O & LDGS PIC
Page Total						
Previous Total						
Total to Date						

DATE 20___	MAKE AND MODEL	ID NUMBER	FROM	TO	LANDINGS		INSTRUMENT APPROACHES			AIRCRAFT CATEGORY AND CLASS						INSTRUMENT		
					DAY	NT	NO.	TYPE & LOCATION		AIRPLANE SINGLE		AIRPLANE MULTI					ACTUAL	SIMULATED (HOOD)	FTD OR SIMULAT

I certify that all information contained in this flight record is true.

Pilot's Signature:

_____

Page Total		
Previous Total		
Total to Date		

NIGHT	CROSS COUNTRY		PIC	SOLO	GROUND TRAINING RECEIVED	FLIGHT TRAINING RECEIVED	FLIGHT TRAINING GIVEN	TOTAL FLIGHT TIME	REMARKS
	ALL	OVER 50 NM							

8710-1 INFORMATION	XC INST'N REC'D	XC SOLO	XC PIC	NIGHT INST'N REC'D	NIGHT PIC	NIGHT T/O & LDGS PIC
Page Total						
Previous Total						
Total to Date						

DATE 20___	MAKE AND MODEL	ID NUMBER	FROM	TO	LANDINGS		INSTRUMENT APPROACHES		AIRCRAFT CATEGORY AND CLASS				INSTRUMENT		
					DAY	NT	NO.	TYPE & LOCATION	AIRPLANE SINGLE	AIRPLANE MULTI			ACTUAL	SIMULATED (HOOD)	FTD OR SIMULATOR

I certify that all information contained in this flight record is true.

Pilot's Signature:

_____

Page Total		
Previous Total		
Total to Date		

60

NIGHT	CROSS COUNTRY		PIC	SOLO	GROUND TRAINING RECEIVED	FLIGHT TRAINING RECEIVED	FLIGHT TRAINING GIVEN	TOTAL FLIGHT TIME	REMARKS
	ALL	OVER 50 NM							

8710-1 INFORMATION	XC INST'N REC'D	XC SOLO	XC PIC	NIGHT INST'N REC'D	NIGHT PIC	NIGHT T/O & LDGS PIC
Page Total						
Previous Total						
Total to Date						

DATE 20___	MAKE AND MODEL	ID NUMBER	FROM	TO	LANDINGS		INSTRUMENT APPROACHES		AIRCRAFT CATEGORY AND CLASS				INSTRUMENT		
					DAY	NT	NO.	TYPE & LOCATION	AIRPLANE SINGLE	AIRPLANE MULTI			ACTUAL	SIMULATED (HOOD)	FTD OR SIMULAT

I certify that all information contained in this flight record is true.

Pilot's Signature:

_____

Page Total			
Previous Total			
Total to Date			

NIGHT	CROSS COUNTRY		PIC	SOLO	GROUND TRAINING RECEIVED	FLIGHT TRAINING RECEIVED	FLIGHT TRAINING GIVEN	TOTAL FLIGHT TIME	REMARKS
	ALL	OVER 50 NM							

8710-1 INFORMATION	XC INST'N REC'D	XC SOLO	XC PIC	NIGHT INST'N REC'D	NIGHT PIC	NIGHT T/O & LDGS PIC
Page Total						
Previous Total						
Total to Date						

DATE 20___	MAKE AND MODEL	ID NUMBER	FROM	TO	LANDINGS		INSTRUMENT APPROACHES		AIRCRAFT CATEGORY AND CLASS				INSTRUMENT		
					DAY	NT	NO.	TYPE & LOCATION	AIRPLANE SINGLE	AIRPLANE MULTI			ACTUAL	SIMULATED (HOOD)	FTD OR SIMULATO
I certify that all information contained in this flight record is true. Pilot's Signature: ___			Page Total												
			Previous Total												
			Total to Date												

NIGHT	CROSS COUNTRY		PIC	SOLO	GROUND TRAINING RECEIVED	FLIGHT TRAINING RECEIVED	FLIGHT TRAINING GIVEN	TOTAL FLIGHT TIME	REMARKS
	ALL	OVER 50 NM							

8710-1 INFORMATION	XC INST'N REC'D	XC SOLO	XC PIC	NIGHT INST'N REC'D	NIGHT PIC	NIGHT T/O & LDGS PIC
Page Total						
Previous Total						
Total to Date						

DATE 20___	MAKE AND MODEL	ID NUMBER	FROM	TO	LANDINGS		INSTRUMENT APPROACHES		AIRCRAFT CATEGORY AND CLASS				INSTRUMENT		
					DAY	NT	NO.	TYPE & LOCATION	AIRPLANE SINGLE	AIRPLANE MULTI			ACTUAL	SIMULATED (HOOD)	FTD OR SIMULATOR
I certify that all information contained in this flight record is true. Pilot's Signature: _____			Page Total												
			Previous Total												
			Total to Date												

| NIGHT | CROSS COUNTRY | | PIC | SOLO | GROUND TRAINING RECEIVED | FLIGHT TRAINING RECEIVED | FLIGHT TRAINING GIVEN | TOTAL FLIGHT TIME | REMARKS |
	ALL	OVER 50 NM							

				8710-1 INFORMATION	XC INST'N REC'D	XC SOLO	XC PIC	NIGHT INST'N REC'D	NIGHT PIC	NIGHT T/O & LDGS PIC
				Page Total						
				Previous Total						
				Total to Date						

DATE 20___	MAKE AND MODEL	ID NUMBER	FROM	TO	LANDINGS		INSTRUMENT APPROACHES		AIRCRAFT CATEGORY AND CLASS				INSTRUMENT		
					DAY	NT	NO.	TYPE & LOCATION	AIRPLANE SINGLE	AIRPLANE MULTI			ACTUAL	SIMULATED (HOOD)	FTD OR SIMULAT
I certify that all information contained in this flight record is true. Pilot's Signature: _____			Page Total												
			Previous Total												
			Total to Date												

NIGHT	CROSS COUNTRY		PIC	SOLO	GROUND TRAINING RECEIVED	FLIGHT TRAINING RECEIVED	FLIGHT TRAINING GIVEN	TOTAL FLIGHT TIME	REMARKS
	ALL	OVER 50 NM							

8710-1 INFORMATION	XC INST'N REC'D	XC SOLO	XC PIC	NIGHT INST'N REC'D	NIGHT PIC	NIGHT T/O & LDGS PIC
Page Total						
Previous Total						
Total to Date						

DATE 20___	MAKE AND MODEL	ID NUMBER	FROM	TO	LANDINGS		INSTRUMENT APPROACHES		AIRCRAFT CATEGORY AND CLASS				INSTRUMENT		
					DAY	NT	NO.	TYPE & LOCATION	AIRPLANE SINGLE	AIRPLANE MULTI			ACTUAL	SIMULATED (HOOD)	FTD OR SIMULAT
I certify that all information contained in this flight record is true. Pilot's Signature: _____			**Page Total**												
			Previous Total												
			Total to Date												

NIGHT	CROSS COUNTRY		PIC	SOLO	GROUND TRAINING RECEIVED	FLIGHT TRAINING RECEIVED	FLIGHT TRAINING GIVEN	TOTAL FLIGHT TIME	REMARKS
	ALL	OVER 50 NM							

8710-1 INFORMATION	XC INST'N REC'D	XC SOLO	XC PIC	NIGHT INST'N REC'D	NIGHT PIC	NIGHT T/O & LDGS PIC
Page Total						
Previous Total						
Total to Date						

DATE 20___	MAKE AND MODEL	ID NUMBER	FROM	TO	LANDINGS		INSTRUMENT APPROACHES		AIRCRAFT CATEGORY AND CLASS				INSTRUMENT		
					DAY	NT	NO.	TYPE & LOCATION	AIRPLANE SINGLE	AIRPLANE MULTI			ACTUAL	SIMULATED (HOOD)	FTD OR SIMULAT
I certify that all information contained in this flight record is true. Pilot's Signature: _____			Page Total												
			Previous Total												
			Total to Date												

NIGHT	CROSS COUNTRY		PIC	SOLO	GROUND TRAINING RECEIVED	FLIGHT TRAINING RECEIVED	FLIGHT TRAINING GIVEN	TOTAL FLIGHT TIME	REMARKS
	ALL	OVER 50 NM							

8710-1 INFORMATION	XC INST'N REC'D	XC SOLO	XC PIC	NIGHT INST'N REC'D	NIGHT PIC	NIGHT T/O & LDGS PIC
Page Total						
Previous Total						
Total to Date						

DATE 20___	MAKE AND MODEL	ID NUMBER	FROM	TO	LANDINGS		INSTRUMENT APPROACHES		AIRCRAFT CATEGORY AND CLASS				INSTRUMENT		
					DAY	NT	NO.	TYPE & LOCATION	AIRPLANE SINGLE	AIRPLANE MULTI			ACTUAL	SIMULATED (HOOD)	FTD OR SIMULAT*
I certify that all information contained in this flight record is true. Pilot's Signature: _____			Page Total												
			Previous Total												
			Total to Date												

74

NIGHT	CROSS COUNTRY		PIC	SOLO	GROUND TRAINING RECEIVED	FLIGHT TRAINING RECEIVED	FLIGHT TRAINING GIVEN	TOTAL FLIGHT TIME	REMARKS
	ALL	OVER 50 NM							

8710-1 INFORMATION	XC INST'N REC'D	XC SOLO	XC PIC	NIGHT INST'N REC'D	NIGHT PIC	NIGHT T/O & LDGS PIC
Page Total						
Previous Total						
Total to Date						

DATE 20___	MAKE AND MODEL	ID NUMBER	FROM	TO	LANDINGS		INSTRUMENT APPROACHES		AIRCRAFT CATEGORY AND CLASS				INSTRUMENT		
					DAY	NT	NO.	TYPE & LOCATION	AIRPLANE SINGLE	AIRPLANE MULTI			ACTUAL	SIMULATED (HOOD)	FTD OR SIMULATO
I certify that all information contained in this flight record is true. Pilot's Signature: _____			Page Total												
			Previous Total												
			Total to Date												

NIGHT	CROSS COUNTRY		PIC	SOLO	GROUND TRAINING RECEIVED	FLIGHT TRAINING RECEIVED	FLIGHT TRAINING GIVEN	TOTAL FLIGHT TIME	REMARKS
	ALL	OVER 50 NM							

8710-1 INFORMATION	XC INST'N REC'D	XC SOLO	XC PIC	NIGHT INST'N REC'D	NIGHT PIC	NIGHT T/O & LDGS PIC
Page Total						
Previous Total						
Total to Date						

DATE 20___	MAKE AND MODEL	ID NUMBER	FROM	TO	LANDINGS		INSTRUMENT APPROACHES		AIRCRAFT CATEGORY AND CLASS				INSTRUMENT		
					DAY	NT	NO.	TYPE & LOCATION	AIRPLANE SINGLE	AIRPLANE MULTI			ACTUAL	SIMULATED (HOOD)	FTD OR SIMULAT
I certify that all information contained in this flight record is true. Pilot's Signature: _____			Page Total												
			Previous Total												
			Total to Date												

78

NIGHT		CROSS COUNTRY				PIC		SOLO		GROUND TRAINING RECEIVED		FLIGHT TRAINING RECEIVED		FLIGHT TRAINING GIVEN		TOTAL FLIGHT TIME		REMARKS
		ALL		OVER 50 NM														

8710-1 INFORMATION	XC INST'N REC'D		XC SOLO		XC PIC		NIGHT INST'N REC'D		NIGHT PIC		NIGHT T/O & LDGS PIC	
Page Total												
Previous Total												
Total to Date												

DATE 20___	MAKE AND MODEL	ID NUMBER	FROM	TO	LANDINGS		INSTRUMENT APPROACHES		AIRCRAFT CATEGORY AND CLASS				INSTRUMENT		
					DAY	NT	NO.	TYPE & LOCATION	AIRPLANE SINGLE	AIRPLANE MULTI			ACTUAL	SIMULATED (HOOD)	FTD OR SIMULAT
I certify that all information contained in this flight record is true. Pilot's Signature: _____			Page Total												
			Previous Total												
			Total to Date												

NIGHT	CROSS COUNTRY		PIC	SOLO	GROUND TRAINING RECEIVED	FLIGHT TRAINING RECEIVED	FLIGHT TRAINING GIVEN	TOTAL FLIGHT TIME	REMARKS
	ALL	OVER 50 NM							

8710-1 INFORMATION	XC INST'N REC'D	XC SOLO	XC PIC	NIGHT INST'N REC'D	NIGHT PIC	NIGHT T/O & LDGS PIC
Page Total						
Previous Total						
Total to Date						

DATE 20___	MAKE AND MODEL	ID NUMBER	FROM	TO	LANDINGS		INSTRUMENT APPROACHES		AIRCRAFT CATEGORY AND CLASS				INSTRUMENT		
					DAY	NT	NO.	TYPE & LOCATION	AIRPLANE SINGLE	AIRPLANE MULTI			ACTUAL	SIMULATED (HOOD)	FTD OR SIMULATO
I certify that all information contained in this flight record is true. Pilot's Signature: _____			Page Total												
			Previous Total												
			Total to Date												

| NIGHT | CROSS COUNTRY | | PIC | SOLO | GROUND TRAINING RECEIVED | FLIGHT TRAINING RECEIVED | FLIGHT TRAINING GIVEN | TOTAL FLIGHT TIME | REMARKS |
	ALL	OVER 50 NM							

8710-1 INFORMATION	XC INST'N REC'D	XC SOLO	XC PIC	NIGHT INST'N REC'D	NIGHT PIC	NIGHT T/O & LDGS PIC
Page Total						
Previous Total						
Total to Date						

DATE 20___	MAKE AND MODEL	ID NUMBER	FROM	TO	LANDINGS		INSTRUMENT APPROACHES		AIRCRAFT CATEGORY AND CLASS				INSTRUMENT		
					DAY	NT	NO.	TYPE & LOCATION	AIRPLANE SINGLE	AIRPLANE MULTI			ACTUAL	SIMULATED (HOOD)	FTD OR SIMULATO
I certify that all information contained in this flight record is true. Pilot's Signature: _____			Page Total												
			Previous Total												
			Total to Date												

NIGHT	CROSS COUNTRY		PIC	SOLO	GROUND TRAINING RECEIVED	FLIGHT TRAINING RECEIVED	FLIGHT TRAINING GIVEN	TOTAL FLIGHT TIME	REMARKS
	ALL	OVER 50 NM							

8710-1 INFORMATION	XC INST'N REC'D	XC SOLO	XC PIC	NIGHT INST'N REC'D	NIGHT PIC	NIGHT T/O & LDGS PIC
Page Total						
Previous Total						
Total to Date						

| DATE 20___ | MAKE AND MODEL | ID NUMBER | FROM | TO | LANDINGS | | INSTRUMENT APPROACHES | | AIRCRAFT CATEGORY AND CLASS | | | | INSTRUMENT | | |
					DAY	NT	NO.	TYPE & LOCATION	AIRPLANE SINGLE	AIRPLANE MULTI			ACTUAL	SIMULATED (HOOD)	FTD OR SIMULATO

I certify that all information contained in this flight record is true. Pilot's Signature: _____	Page Total												
	Previous Total												
	Total to Date												

NIGHT	CROSS COUNTRY		PIC	SOLO	GROUND TRAINING RECEIVED	FLIGHT TRAINING RECEIVED	FLIGHT TRAINING GIVEN	TOTAL FLIGHT TIME	REMARKS
	ALL	OVER 50 NM							

8710-1 INFORMATION	XC INST'N REC'D	XC SOLO	XC PIC	NIGHT INST'N REC'D	NIGHT PIC	NIGHT T/O & LDGS PIC
Page Total						
Previous Total						
Total to Date						

DATE 20___	MAKE AND MODEL	ID NUMBER	FROM	TO	LANDINGS		INSTRUMENT APPROACHES		AIRCRAFT CATEGORY AND CLASS				INSTRUMENT		
					DAY	NT	NO.	TYPE & LOCATION	AIRPLANE SINGLE	AIRPLANE MULTI			ACTUAL	SIMULATED (HOOD)	FTD OR SIMULATO

I certify that all information contained in this flight record is true.

Pilot's Signature:

_____

Page Total		
Previous Total		
Total to Date		

NIGHT	CROSS COUNTRY		PIC	SOLO	GROUND TRAINING RECEIVED	FLIGHT TRAINING RECEIVED	FLIGHT TRAINING GIVEN	TOTAL FLIGHT TIME	REMARKS
	ALL	OVER 50 NM							

8710-1 INFORMATION	XC INST'N REC'D	XC SOLO	XC PIC	NIGHT INST'N REC'D	NIGHT PIC	NIGHT T/O & LDGS PIC
Page Total						
Previous Total						
Total to Date						

GROUND INSTRUCTION

DATE	SUBJECTS COVERED	INSTRUCTOR SIGNATURE	TIME THIS SESSION		TOTAL TIME

	GROUND INSTRUCTION					
DATE	SUBJECTS COVERED	INSTRUCTOR SIGNATURE	TIME THIS SESSION		TOTAL TIME	

GROUND INSTRUCTION

DATE	SUBJECTS COVERED	INSTRUCTOR SIGNATURE	TIME THIS SESSION		TOTAL TIME

GROUND INSTRUCTION

DATE	SUBJECTS COVERED	INSTRUCTOR SIGNATURE	TIME THIS SESSION		TOTAL TIME	

LIST OF ENDORSEMENTS

Presolo aeronautical knowledge: § 61.87(b)	**Presolo flight training: § 61.87(c)**	**Solo flight (first 90-day period): § 61.87(n)**
I certify that _____ (First Name, MI, Last Name) has satisfactorily completed the presolo knowledge test required by § 61.87(b) for the _____ (aircraft make and model).	I certify that _____ (First Name, MI, Last Name) has received the required presolo flight training in a _____ (aircraft make and model). I have determined that (he or she) has demonstrated satisfactory proficiency and safety on the maneuvers and procedures required by § 61.87 in this or similar make and model of aircraft to be flown. Limitations: _____ _____	I certify that _____ (First Name, MI, Last Name) has received the required training to qualify for solo flying. I have determined (he or she) meets the applicable requirements of § 61.87(n) and is proficient to make solo flights in a _____ (aircraft make and model). Limitations: _____ _____
Signed _____ Date _____ CFI # _____ Exp Date _____	Signed _____ Date _____ CFI # _____ Exp Date _____	Signed _____ Date _____ CFI # _____ Exp Date _____
Solo flight (additional 90-day period): § 61.87(p)	**Solo flight (additional 90-day period): § 61.87(p)**	**Solo flight (additional 90-day period): § 61.87(p)**
I certify that _____ (First Name, MI, Last Name) has received the required training to qualify for solo flight. I have determined that (he or she) meets the applicable requirements of § 61.87(p) and is proficient to make solo flights in a _____ (aircraft make and model). Limitations: _____ _____	I certify that _____ (First Name, MI, Last Name) has received the required training to qualify for solo flight. I have determined that (he or she) meets the applicable requirements of § 61.87(p) and is proficient to make solo flights in a _____ (aircraft make and model). Limitations: _____ _____	I certify that _____ (First Name, MI, Last Name) has received the required training to qualify for solo flight. I have determined that (he or she) meets the applicable requirements of § 61.87(p) and is proficient to make solo flights in a _____ (aircraft make and model). Limitations: _____ _____
Signed _____ Date _____ CFI # _____ Exp Date _____	Signed _____ Date _____ CFI # _____ Exp Date _____	Signed _____ Date _____ CFI # _____ Exp Date _____

Initial solo cross-country flight:
§ 61.93(c)(1) and (2)

I certify that _____
(First Name, MI, Last Name) has received the required solo cross-country training. I find that (he or she) has met the applicable requirements of § 61.93, and is proficient to make solo cross-country flights in a _____ (aircraft make and model) (aircraft category).

Signed _____ Date _____
CFI # _____ Exp Date _____

Solo cross-country flight: § 61.93(c)(2)(ii)

I have reviewed the cross-country planning of
_____
(First Name, MI, Last Name). I find the planning and preparation to be correct to make the solo flight from _____ (location) to _____ (location) via _____ (route of flight) with landings at _____ (names of airports) in a _____ (aircraft make and model) on _____ (date).

Limitations: _____
_____

Signed _____ Date _____
CFI # _____ Exp Date _____

Solo cross-country flight: § 61.93(c)(2)(ii)

I have reviewed the cross-country planning of
_____
(First Name, MI, Last Name). I find the planning and preparation to be correct to make the solo flight from _____ (location) to _____ (location) via _____ (route of flight) with landings at _____ (names of airports) in a _____ (aircraft make and model) on _____ (date).

Limitations: _____
_____

Signed _____ Date _____
CFI # _____ Exp Date _____

Solo cross-country flight: § 61.93(c)(2)(ii)

I have reviewed the cross-country planning of
_____
(First Name, MI, Last Name). I find the planning and preparation to be correct to make the solo flight from _____ (location) to _____ (location) via _____ (route of flight) with landings at _____ (names of airports) in a _____ (aircraft make and model) on _____ (date).

Limitations: _____

Signed _____ Date _____
CFI # _____ Exp Date _____

Solo cross-country flight: § 61.93(c)(2)(ii)

I have reviewed the cross-country planning of
_____
(First Name, MI, Last Name). I find the planning and preparation to be correct to make the solo flight from _____ (location) to _____ (location) via _____ (route of flight) with landings at _____ (names of airports) in a _____ (aircraft make and model) on _____ (date).

Limitations: _____

Signed _____ Date _____
CFI # _____ Exp Date _____

Repeated solo cross-country flights less than 50 NM from the point of departure: § 61.93(b)(2)

I certify that _____
(First Name, MI, Last Name) has received the required training in both directions between and at both _____
(airport names). I have determined that (he or she) is proficient to conduct repeated solo cross-country flights over that route as required by § 61.93(b)(2).

Limitations: _____

Signed _____ Date _____
CFI # _____ Exp Date _____

Solo takeoffs and landings at another airport within 25 NM: § 61.93(b)(1)	Solo takeoffs and landings at another airport within 25 NM: § 61.93(b)(1)	Presolo flight training at night (valid for a 90-day period): § 61.87(c) and (o)
I certify that _____ (First Name, MI, Last Name) has received the training required by § 61.93(b)(1). I have determined that (he or she) is proficient to practice solo takeoffs and landings at _____ (airport name). Limitations: _____ _____ Signed _____ Date _____ CFI # _____ Exp Date _____	I certify that _____ (First Name, MI, Last Name) has received the training required by § 61.93(b)(1). I have determined that (he or she) is proficient to practice solo takeoffs and landings at _____ (airport name). Limitations: _____ _____ Signed _____ Date _____ CFI # _____ Exp Date _____	I certify that _____ (First Name, MI, Last Name) has received the required presolo training in a _____ (aircraft make and model). I have determined that (he or she) has demonstrated proficiency in the maneuvers and procedures required by § 61.87(o) and is proficient to make solo flights at night in a _____ (aircraft make and model). Limitations: _____ _____ Signed _____ Date _____ CFI # _____ Exp Date _____
Solo flight in Class B airspace (valid for a 90-day period): § 61.95(a)	Solo flight to, from, or at an airport located in Class B airspace (valid for a 90-day period): §§ 61.95(b) and 91.131(b)(1)	Solo flight to, from, or at an airport located in Class B airspace (valid for a 90-day period): §§ 61.95(b) and 91.131(b)(1)
I certify that _____ (First Name, MI, Last Name) has received the training required by § 61.95(a). I have determined that (he or she) is proficient to conduct solo flights in _____ (name of Class B area) airspace. Limitations: _____ Signed _____ Date _____ CFI # _____ Exp Date _____	I certify that _____ (First Name, MI, Last Name) has received the training required by § 61.95(b)(1). I have determined that (he or she) is proficient to conduct solo flight operations at (name of airport) _____. Limitations: _____ _____ Signed _____ Date _____ CFI # _____ Exp Date _____	I certify that _____ (First Name, MI, Last Name) has received the training required by § 61.95(b)(1). I have determined that (he or she) is proficient to conduct solo flight operations at (name of airport) _____. Limitations: _____ _____ Signed _____ Date _____ CFI # _____ Exp Date _____

Private pilot aeronautical knowledge test:
§§ 61.35(a)(1), 61.103(d), and 61.105

I certify that _____
(First Name, MI, Last Name) has received the
required training in accordance with § 61.105. I have
determined (he or she) is prepared for the _____
_____ (name of) knowledge test.

Signed _____ Date _____
CFI # _____ Exp Date _____

Prerequisites for practical test:
§ 61.39(a)(6)(i)(ii) and (iii)

I certify that _____
(First Name, MI, Last Name) has received and logged
training time within 2 calendar-months preceding the
month of application in preparation for the practical
test and (he or she) is prepared for the required
practical test for issuance of _____
(applicable) certificate. I also certify that (he or she)
has demonstrated satisfactory knowledge of the
subject areas in which (he or she) was deficient on
the _____ (applicable) airman knowledge
test.

Signed _____ Date _____
CFI # _____ Exp Date _____

Private pilot practical test: §§ 61.103(f), 61.107(b),
and 61.109

I certify that _____
(First Name, MI, Last Name) has received the training
required by §§ 61.107 and 61.109. I have determined
that (he or she) is prepared for the _____
_____ (name of practical test)
practical test.

Signed _____ Date _____
CFI # _____ Exp Date _____

Instrument rating aeronautical knowledge test:
§§ 61.35(a)(1) and 61.65(a) and (b)

I certify that _____
(First Name, MI, Last Name) has received the
required training of § 61.65(b). I have determined that
(he or she) is prepared for the Instrument–(airplane,
helicopter, or powered-lift) knowledge test.

Signed _____ Date _____
CFI # _____ Exp Date _____

Prerequisites for instrument practical test:
§ 61.39(a)

I certify that _____
(First Name, MI, Last Name) has received and logged
the required flight time/training of § 61.39(a) in
preparation for the practical test within 2 calendar-
months preceding the date of the test and has
satisfactory knowledge of the subject areas in which
(he or she) was shown to be deficient by the FAA
airman knowledge test report. I have determined
(he or she) is prepared for the Instrument–(airplane,
helicopter, or powered-lift) practical test.

Signed _____ Date _____
CFI # _____ Exp Date _____

Instrument rating practical test: § 61.65(a)(6)

I certify that _____
(First Name, MI, Last Name) has received the training
required by § 61.65(c) and (d). I have determined that
(he or she) is prepared for the Instrument–(airplane,
helicopter, or powered-lift) knowledge test.

Signed _____ Date _____
CFI # _____ Exp Date _____

Commercial pilot aeronautical knowledge test: § 61.35(a)(1), 61.123(c), and 61.125	Prerequisites for practical test: § 61.39(a)(6)(i)(ii) and (iii)	Commercial pilot practical test: §§ 61.123(e), 61.127, and 61.129
I certify that _____ (First Name, MI, Last Name) has received the required training of § 61.125. I have determined that (he or she) is prepared for the _____ (name of) knowledge test.	I certify that _____ (First Name, MI, Last Name) has received and logged training time within 2 calendar-months preceding the month of application in preparation for the practical test and (he or she) is prepared for the required practical test for issuance of _____ (applicable) certificate. I also certify that (he or she) has demonstrated satisfactory knowledge of the subject areas in which (he or she) was deficient on the _____ (applicable) airman knowledge test.	I certify that _____ (First Name, MI, Last Name) has received the training required by §§ 61.127 and 61.129. I have determined that (he or she) is prepared for the _____ (name of practical test) practical test.
Signed _____ Date _____ CFI # _____ Exp Date _____	Signed _____ Date _____ CFI # _____ Exp Date _____	Signed _____ Date _____ CFI # _____ Exp Date _____
Fundamentals of instructing: §§ 61.183(d) and 61.185(a)(1)	Prerequisites for practical test: § 61.39(a)(6)(i)(ii) and (iii)	Flight instructor practical test: §§ 61.183(g) and 61.187(a) and (b)
I certify that _____ (First Name, MI, Last Name) has received the fundamentals of instruction training required by § 61.185(a)(1).	I certify that _____ (First Name, MI, Last Name) has received and logged training time within 2 calendar-months preceding the month of application in preparation for the practical test and (he or she) is prepared for the required practical test for issuance of _____ (applicable) certificate. I also certify that (he or she) has demonstrated satisfactory knowledge of the subject areas in which (he or she) was deficient on the _____ (applicable) airman knowledge test.	I certify that _____ (First Name, MI, Last Name) has received the training required by § 61.187(b). I have determined that (he or she) is prepared for the CFI – _____ (aircraft category and class) practical test.
Signed _____ Date _____ CFI # _____ Exp Date _____	Signed _____ Date _____ CFI # _____ Exp Date _____	Signed _____ Date _____ CFI # _____ Exp Date _____

Spin training: § 61.183(i)(1)

I certify that _____
(First Name, MI, Last Name) has received the training required by § 61.183(i). I have determined that (he or she) is competent and proficient in instructional skills for training stall awareness, spin entry, spins, and spin recovery procedures.

Signed _____ Date _____
CFI # _____ Exp Date _____

Prerequisites for practical test: § 61.39(a)(6)(i)(ii) and (iii)

I certify that _____
(First Name, MI, Last Name) has received and logged training time within 2 calendar-months preceding the month of application in preparation for the practical test and (he or she) is prepared for the required practical test for issuance of _____
(applicable) certificate. I also certify that (he or she) has demonstrated satisfactory knowledge of the subject areas in which (he or she) was deficient on the _____ (applicable) airman knowledge test.

Signed _____ Date _____
CFI # _____ Exp Date _____

Flight instructor–instrument practical test: §§ 61.183(g) and 61.187(a) and (b)(7)

I certify that _____
(First Name, MI, Last Name) has received the CFII training required by § 61.187(b)(7). I have determined that (he or she) is prepared for the CFII – _____
_____
(airplane, helicopter, or powered-lift) practical test.

Signed _____ Date _____
CFI # _____ Exp Date _____

Prerequisites for practical test: § 61.39(a)(6)(i)(ii) and (iii)

I certify that _____
(First Name, MI, Last Name) has received and logged training time within 2 calendar-months preceding the month of application in preparation for the practical test and (he or she) is prepared for the required practical test for issuance of _____
(applicable) certificate. I also certify that (he or she) has demonstrated satisfactory knowledge of the subject areas in which (he or she) was deficient on the _____ (applicable) airman knowledge test.

Signed _____ Date _____
CFI # _____ Exp Date _____

Additional aircraft category or class rating: § 61.63(b) or (c)

I certify that _____
_____ (First Name, MI, Last Name, pilot certificate, certificate number), has received the required training for an additional
_____
(aircraft category/class) rating. I have determined that (he or she) is prepared for the _____
(name of practical test) practical test for the addition of a _____ (aircraft category/class) rating.

Signed _____ Date _____
CFI # _____ Exp Date _____

PIC in a complex airplane: § 61.31(e)

I certify that _____
_____ (First Name, MI, Last Name, pilot certificate, certificate number), has received the training required by § 61.31(e) in a
_____
(make and model of complex airplane). I have determined that (he or she) is proficient in the operation and systems of a complex airplane.

Signed _____ Date _____
CFI # _____ Exp Date _____

PIC in a high performance airplane: § 61.31(f)	PIC in a tailwheel airplane: § 61.31(i)	PIC in a pressurized aircraft capable of high altitude operations: § 61.31(g)
I certify that _____ _____ (First Name, MI, Last Name, pilot certificate, certificate number), has received the training required by § 61.31(f) in a _____ (make and model of high performance airplane). I have determined that (he or she) is proficient in the operation and systems of a high performance airplane. Signed _____ Date _____ CFI # _____ Exp Date _____	I certify that _____ _____ (First Name, MI, Last Name, pilot certificate, certificate number), has received the training required by § 61.31(i) in a _____ (make and model of tailwheel airplane). I have determined that (he or she) is proficient in the operation of a tailwheel airplane. Signed _____ Date _____ CFI # _____ Exp Date _____	I certify that _____ _____ (First Name, MI, Last Name, pilot certificate, certificate number), has received the training required by § 61.31(g) in a _____ (make and model of pressurized aircraft). I have determined that (he or she) is proficient in the operation and systems of a pressurized aircraft. Signed _____ Date _____ CFI # _____ Exp Date _____
Completion of a phase of an FAA-sponsored pilot proficiency award program (WINGS): § 61.56(e)	Completion of a phase of an FAA-sponsored pilot proficiency award program (WINGS): § 61.56(e)	Completion of a phase of an FAA-sponsored pilot proficiency award program (WINGS): § 61.56(e)
I certify that _____ _____ (First Name, MI, Last Name, grade of pilot certificate, certificate number), has satisfactorily completed Level: (Basic/Advanced/Master), Phase No. ____ of a WINGS program on _____ (date). Signed _____ Date _____ CFI # _____ Exp Date _____	I certify that _____ _____ (First Name, MI, Last Name, grade of pilot certificate, certificate number), has satisfactorily completed Level: (Basic/Advanced/Master), Phase No. ____ of a WINGS program on _____ (date). Signed _____ Date _____ CFI # _____ Exp Date _____	I certify that _____ _____ (First Name, MI, Last Name, grade of pilot certificate, certificate number), has satisfactorily completed Level: (Basic/Advanced/Master), Phase No. ____ of a WINGS program on _____ (date). Signed _____ Date _____ CFI # _____ Exp Date _____

Instrument proficiency check: § 61.57(d)

I certify that _____
_____ (First Name, MI, Last
Name, pilot certificate, certificate number), has satisfactorily completed the instrument proficiency check
required by § 61.57(d) in a _____
(aircraft make and model).

Signed _____ Date _____
CFI # _____ Exp Date _____

Instrument proficiency check: § 61.57(d)

I certify that _____
_____ (First Name, MI, Last
Name, pilot certificate, certificate number), has satisfactorily completed the instrument proficiency check
required by § 61.57(d) in a _____
(aircraft make and model).

Signed _____ Date _____
CFI # _____ Exp Date _____

Instrument proficiency check: § 61.57(d)

I certify that _____
_____ (First Name, MI, Las
Name, pilot certificate, certificate number), has satisfactorily completed the instrument proficiency check
required by § 61.57(d) in a _____
(aircraft make and model).

Signed _____ Date _____
CFI # _____ Exp Date _____

Instrument proficiency check: § 61.57(d)

I certify that _____
_____ (First Name, MI, Last
Name, pilot certificate, certificate number), has satisfactorily completed the instrument proficiency check
required by § 61.57(d) in a _____
(aircraft make and model).

Signed _____ Date _____
CFI # _____ Exp Date _____

Instrument proficiency check: § 61.57(d)

I certify that _____
_____ (First Name, MI, Last
Name, pilot certificate, certificate number), has satisfactorily completed the instrument proficiency check
required by § 61.57(d) in a _____
(aircraft make and model).

Signed _____ Date _____
CFI # _____ Exp Date _____

Instrument proficiency check: § 61.57(d)

I certify that _____
_____ (First Name, MI, Las
Name, pilot certificate, certificate number), has satisfactorily completed the instrument proficiency check
required by § 61.57(d) in a _____
(aircraft make and model).

Signed _____ Date _____
CFI # _____ Exp Date _____

Completion of a flight review: § 61.56(a) and (c)

I certify that _____
_____ (First Name, MI, Last
Name, pilot certificate, certificate number), has
satisfactorily completed the flight review of § 61.56(a)
on _____ (date).

Signed _____ Date _____
CFI # _____ Exp Date _____

Completion of a flight review: § 61.56(a) and (c)

I certify that _____
_____ (First Name, MI, Last
Name, pilot certificate, certificate number), has
satisfactorily completed the flight review of § 61.56(a)
on _____ (date).

Signed _____ Date _____
CFI # _____ Exp Date _____

Completion of a flight review: § 61.56(a) and (c)

I certify that _____
_____ (First Name, MI, Last
Name, pilot certificate, certificate number), has
satisfactorily completed the flight review of § 61.56(a)
on _____ (date).

Signed _____ Date _____
CFI # _____ Exp Date _____

Completion of a flight review: § 61.56(a) and (c)

I certify that _____
_____ (First Name, MI, Last
Name, pilot certificate, certificate number), has
satisfactorily completed the flight review of § 61.56(a)
on _____ (date).

Signed _____ Date _____
CFI # _____ Exp Date _____

Completion of a flight review: § 61.56(a) and (c)

I certify that _____
_____ (First Name, MI, Last
Name, pilot certificate, certificate number), has
satisfactorily completed the flight review of § 61.56(a)
on _____ (date).

Signed _____ Date _____
CFI # _____ Exp Date _____

Completion of a flight review: § 61.56(a) and (c)

I certify that _____
_____ (First Name, MI, Last
Name, pilot certificate, certificate number), has
satisfactorily completed the flight review of § 61.56(a)
on _____ (date).

Signed _____ Date _____
CFI # _____ Exp Date _____

<table>
<tr><td>

Sport pilot solo flight (first 90-day period): § 61.87(n)

I certify that _____
(First Name, MI, Last Name) has received the training required to qualify for solo flight. I have determined that (he or she) meets the applicable requirements of § 61.87(n) and is proficient to make solo flights in a

_____
(aircraft make and model).

Signed _____ Date _____
CFI # _____ Exp Date _____

</td><td>

Solo flight to, from, or at an airport located in Class B, C, or D airspace or an airport having an operating control tower (valid for a 90-day period): §§ 61.94(a)(1) and 91.131(b)(1)

I certify that _____
(First Name, MI, Last Name) has received the training required by § 61.94(a). I have determined that (he or she) is proficient to conduct solo flights at

_____
(name of airport) located in Class B, C, or D airspace or at an airport having an operational control tower.

Limitations: _____

Signed _____ Date _____
CFI # _____ Exp Date _____

</td><td>

Solo flight in Class B, C, or D airspace (valid for a 90-day period): § 61.94(a)

I certify that _____
(First Name, MI, Last Name) has received the training required by § 61.94(a). I have determined that (he or she) is proficient to conduct solo flights in
_____ (name of Class B, C, or D) airspace and is authorized to operate to, from, through, and at _____ airport.

Limitations: _____

Signed _____ Date _____
CFI # _____ Exp Date _____

</td></tr>
<tr><td>

Sport pilot aeronautical knowledge test: §§ 61.35(a)(1) and 61.309

I certify that _____
(First Name, MI, Last Name) has received the training and possesses the knowledge required by §§ 61.35(a)(1) and 61.309. I trained (him or her) or evaluated (his or her) home study course materials, and I have determined that (he or she) is prepared for the Sport Pilot Knowledge Test.

Signed _____ Date _____
CFI # _____ Exp Date _____

</td><td>

Taking sport pilot practical test: §§ 61.309, 61.311, and 61.313

I certify that _____
(First Name, MI, Last Name) has received the training required by §§ 61.309 and 61.311 and met the aeronautical experience requirements of § 61.313. I have determined that (he or she) is prepared for the Sport Pilot Practical Test.

Signed _____ Date _____
CFI # _____ Exp Date _____

</td><td>

Passing sport pilot practical test: §§ 61.309, 61.311, and 61.313

NOTE: Required by § 61.317, issued by a Sport Pilot Examiner (SPE)

I certify that _____
(First Name, MI, Last Name) has met the requirements of §§ 61.309, 61.311, and 61.313, and have determined that (he or she) is proficient to act as PIC of a _____
(category and class of) light sport aircraft.

Signed _____ Date _____
CFI # _____ Exp Date _____

</td></tr>
</table>

<table>
<tr>
<td>

...aking flight proficiency check for different category or class of aircraft: §§ 61.309 and 61.311

...certify that _____ (First Name, MI, Last Name) has received the training ...quired by §§ 61.309 and 61.311. I have determined ...at (he or she) is prepared for the _____ _____ (name of proficiency check).

...igned _____ Date _____
...FI # _____ Exp Date _____

</td>
<td>

Passing flight proficiency check for different category or class of aircraft: §§ 61.309 and 61.311

I certify that _____ (First Name, MI, Last Name) has met the requirements of §§ 61.309 and 61.311, and I have determined that (he or she) is proficient to act as PIC of _____ (category and class) of light-sport aircraft.

Signed _____ Date _____
CFI # _____ Exp Date _____

</td>
<td>

Passing flight proficiency check for different category or class of aircraft: §§ 61.309 and 61.311

I certify that _____ (First Name, MI, Last Name) has met the requirements of §§ 61.309 and 61.311, and I have determined that (he or she) is proficient to act as PIC of _____ (category and class) of light-sport aircraft.

Signed _____ Date _____
CFI # _____ Exp Date _____

</td>
</tr>
<tr>
<td>

...light in a light-sport aircraft that has a V_H greater ...an 87 knots CAS: § 61.327

...certify that _____ (First Name, MI, Last Name) has received the training ...quired by § 61.327 in a _____ ...ircraft make and model). I have determined that (he ...° she) is proficient to act as PIC of a light-sport ...rcraft that has a V_H greater than 87 knots CAS.

...gned _____ Date _____
...FI # _____ Exp Date _____

</td>
<td>

Light-sport aircraft that has a V_H less than or equal to 87 knots CAS: § 61.327

I certify that _____ (First Name, MI, Last Name) has received the required training required in accordance with § 61.327(a) in a _____ (aircraft make and model). I have determined (him or her) proficient to act as pilot in command of a light-sport aircraft that has a V_H less than or equal to 87 knots CAS.

Signed _____ Date _____
CFI # _____ Exp Date _____

</td>
<td>

Flight in Class B, C, or D airspace, at an airport located in Class B, C, or D airspace, or to, from, through, or at an airport having an operational control tower: § 61.325

I certify that _____ (First Name, MI, Last Name) has received the training required by § 61.325. I have determined that (he or she) is proficient to conduct operations in Class B, C, or D airspace, at an airport located in Class B, C, or D airspace, or to, from, through, or at an airport having an operational control tower.

Signed _____ Date _____
CFI # _____ Exp Date _____

</td>
</tr>
</table>

Fundamentals of instructing knowledge test: §§ 61.405(a)(1) and 61.407

I certify that _____
(First Name, MI, Last Name) has received the training and possesses the knowledge required by § 61.407. I trained (him or her) or evaluated (his or her) home study course materials, and I have determined that (he or she) is prepared for the Fundamentals of Instructing Knowledge Test.

Signed _____ Date _____
CFI # _____ Exp Date _____

Taking the flight instructor practical test: §§ 61.405(b), 61.409, and 61.411

I certify that _____
(First Name, MI, Last Name) has received the training required by § 61.409 and met the aeronautical experience required by § 61.411. I have determined that (he or she) is prepared for the flight instructor with a sport pilot rating practical test in a _____

_____
(aircraft category and class).

Signed _____ Date _____
CFI # _____ Exp Date _____

Passing the flight instructor practical test: §§ 61.409 and 61.411

NOTE: Required by § 61.417, issued by a DPE

I certify that _____
(First Name, MI, Last Name) has met the requirements of §§ 61.409 and 61.411. I have determined that (he or she) is proficient and authorized for the _____
(aircraft category and class) flight instructor with a sport pilot rating privilege.

Signed _____ Date _____
CFI # _____ Exp Date _____

Sport pilot flight instructor aeronautical knowledge test: §§ 61.35(a)(1), 61.405(a), and 61.407

I certify that _____
(First Name, MI, Last Name) has received the training and possesses the knowledge required by § 61.407. I trained (him or her) or evaluated (his or her) home study course materials, and I have determined that (he or she) is prepared for the Sport Pilot Flight Instructor Knowledge Test.

Signed _____ Date _____
CFI # _____ Exp Date _____

Taking the flight instructor flight proficiency check to provide training in a different category or class of aircraft (additional category/class): §§ 61.409 and 61.419

I certify that _____
(First Name, MI, Last Name) has received the training required by § 61.409 and 61.419. I have determined that (he or she) is prepared for a proficiency check as a flight instructor with a sport pilot rating in a _____

_____
(aircraft category and class).

Signed _____ Date _____
CFI # _____ Exp Date _____

Passing the flight instructor flight proficiency check to provide training in a different category class of aircraft (additional category/class): §§ 61.409 and 61.419

I certify that _____
(First Name, MI, Last Name) has met the requiremen of § 61.409 and 61.419. I have determined that (he o she) is proficient and authorized for the additional

_____
(aircraft category and class) flight instructor privilege

Signed _____ Date _____
CFI # _____ Exp Date _____

Sport pilot instructor to train sport pilots on flight by reference to instruments: § 61.412	Spin training: § 61.405(b)(1)(ii)	Act as PIC without category, class, and rating: § 61.31(d)(2)
I certify that I have given _____ (First Name, MI, Last Name) 3 hours of flight training and 1 hour of ground instruction specific to providing flight training on control and maneuvering an airplane solely by reference to the instruments in accordance with § 61.412. I have determined that (he or she) is proficient and authorized to provide training on control and maneuvering an airplane solely by reference to the flight instruments to this instructor's sport pilot candidate, who intends to operate an LSA airplane with V$_H$ greater than 87 KCAS on a cross-country flight.	I certify that _____ (First Name, MI, Last Name) has received the training required by § 61.405(b)(1)(ii). I have determined that (he or she) is competent and possesses instructional proficiency in stall awareness, spin entry, spins, and spin recovery procedures.	I certify that _____ _____ (First Name, MI, Last Name, pilot certificate, certificate number) has received the training required by § 61.31(d)(2) to serve as PIC in a _____ (aircraft category and class). I have determined that (he or she) is prepared to solo that _____ _____ (aircraft make and model).
Signed _____ Date _____ FI # _____ Exp Date _____	Signed _____ Date _____ CFI # _____ Exp Date _____	Signed _____ Date _____ CFI # _____ Exp Date _____
TSA Security Endorsement	**TSA Security Endorsement**	**TSA Security Endorsement**
I certify that _____ (insert student's name) has presented me a _____ (insert type of document presented, such as a U.S. birth certificate or U.S. passport) _____ (the relevant control or sequential number on the document, if any) establishing that (he or she) is a U.S. citizen or national in accordance with 49 CFR 1552.3(h).	I certify that _____ (insert student's name) has presented me a _____ (insert type of document presented, such as a U.S. birth certificate or U.S. passport) _____ (the relevant control or sequential number on the document, if any) establishing that (he or she) is a U.S. citizen or national in accordance with 49 CFR 1552.3(h).	I certify that _____ (insert student's name) has presented me a _____ (insert type of document presented, such as a U.S. birth certificate or U.S. passport) _____ (the relevant control or sequential number on the document, if any) establishing that (he or she) is a U.S. citizen or national in accordance with 49 CFR 1552.3(h).
Signed _____ Date _____ FI # _____ Exp Date _____	Signed _____ Date _____ CFI # _____ Exp Date _____	Signed _____ Date _____ CFI # _____ Exp Date _____

Review of a home study curriculum: § 61.35(a)(1)

I certify that I have reviewed the home study curriculum of _____
(First Name, MI, Last Name). I have determined that (he or she) is prepared for the _____
(name of knowledge test).

Signed _____ Date _____
CFI # _____ Exp Date _____

Review of a home study curriculum: § 61.35(a)(1)

I certify that I have reviewed the home study curriculum of _____
(First Name, MI, Last Name). I have determined that (he or she) is prepared for the _____
(name of knowledge test).

Signed _____ Date _____
CFI # _____ Exp Date _____

Review of a home study curriculum: § 61.35(a)(1)

I certify that I have reviewed the home study curriculum of _____
(First Name, MI, Last Name). I have determined that (he or she) is prepared for the _____
(name of knowledge test).

Signed _____ Date _____
CFI # _____ Exp Date _____

Ground instructor who does not meet the recent experience requirements: § 61.217(b)

NOTE: Signed by CFI or CGI, as appropriate; the expiration date would apply only to a CFI.

I certify that _____
(First Name, MI, Last Name) has demonstrated satisfactory proficiency on the appropriate ground instructor knowledge and training subjects of § 61.213(a)(3) and (a)(4).

Signed _____ Date _____
CFI # _____ Exp Date _____

Ground instructor who does not meet the recent experience requirements: § 61.217(b)

NOTE: Signed by CFI or CGI, as appropriate; the expiration date would apply only to a CFI.

I certify that _____
(First Name, MI, Last Name) has demonstrated satisfactory proficiency on the appropriate ground instructor knowledge and training subjects of § 61.213(a)(3) and (a)(4).

Signed _____ Date _____
CFI # _____ Exp Date _____

Retesting after failure of a knowledge or practical test: § 61.49

NOTE: The instructor must sign the block provided for the instructor's recommendation on the reverse side of FAA Form 8710-1 application for each retake of a practical test.

I certify that _____
(First Name, MI, Last Name) has received the additional (flight and/or ground, as appropriate) training as required by § 61.49. I have determined that (he or she) is prepared for the _____
(name of knowledge/practical test).

Signed _____ Date _____
CFI # _____ Exp Date _____

MISCELLANEOUS

MISCELLANEOUS

MISCELLANEOUS

MISCELLANEOUS